T0417878

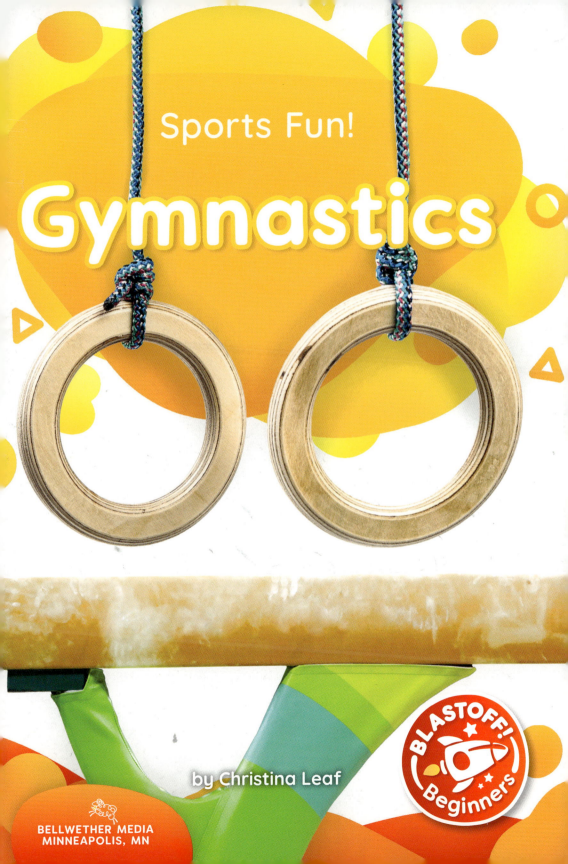

Sports Fun!

Gymnastics

by Christina Leaf

BELLWETHER MEDIA
MINNEAPOLIS, MN

BLASTOFF!
Beginners

Blastoff! Beginners are developed by literacy experts and educators to meet the needs of early readers. These engaging informational texts support young children as they begin reading about their world. Through simple language and high frequency words paired with crisp, colorful photos, Blastoff! Beginners launch young readers into the universe of independent reading.

Blastoff! Universe ★

Reading Level — Grade K

Grades 1-3

Grade 4

Sight Words in This Book 🔍

a	for	people	we
and	jump	some	
are	many	the	
at	may	there	
be	on	they	
do	one	two	

This edition first published in 2024 by Bellwether Media, Inc.

No part of this publication may be reproduced in whole or in part without written permission of the publisher. For information regarding permission, write to Bellwether Media, Inc., Attention: Permissions Department, 6012 Blue Circle Drive, Minnetonka, MN 55343.

Library of Congress Cataloging-in-Publication Data

Names: Leaf, Christina, author.
Title: Gymnastics / by Christina Leaf.
Description: Minneapolis, MN : Bellwether Media, Inc., 2024. | Series: Blastoff! Beginners: Sports fun! | Includes bibliographical references and index. | Audience: Ages 4-7 | Audience: Grades K-1
Identifiers: LCCN 2023004966 (print) | LCCN 2023004967 (ebook) | ISBN 9798886873948 (library binding) | ISBN 9798886875829 (ebook)
Subjects: LCSH: Gymnastics--Juvenile literature.
Classification: LCC GV461.3 .L42 2024 (print) | LCC GV461.3 (ebook) | DDC 796.44--dc23/eng/20230202
LC record available at https://lccn.loc.gov/2023004966
LC ebook record available at https://lccn.loc.gov/2023004967

Editor: Rebecca Sabelko   Designer: Jeffrey Kollock

Printed in the United States of America, North Mankato, MN.

Table of Contents

Flips and Jumps

People do flips and jumps.
We love gymnastics!

What Is Gymnastics?

Gymnasts show strength. They show **balance**.

Gymnasts may be **solo** or on a team. They try for points.

At the Gym

Gymnasts work at a gym. They wear tight clothes.

gym

There are many **events**. Some are for girls. Some are for boys.

Girls swing
on two bars.
Boys swing
on one bar.

Girls balance
on the **beam**.
Boys flip
on the rings.

rings

beam

Girls and boys
do moves
on the floor.

floor

They wait for
a score.
The highest
score wins!

Gymnastics Facts

Doing Gymnastics

tight clothes

gym

bars

Gymnastic Events

bars

beam

rings

Glossary

balance

the act of
staying steady

beam

a long,
thin object

events

exercises that
gymnasts do

solo

alone

23

To Learn More

ON THE WEB

FACTSURFER

Factsurfer.com gives you a safe, fun way to find more information.

1. Go to www.factsurfer.com.

2. Enter "gymnastics" into the search box and click 🔍.

3. Select your book cover to see a list of related content.

Index